T0375604

Victory
over Anger

*An
autobiography
testimony of
God's salvation*

James Dean Anderson

WESTBOW
P R E S S®
A DIVISION OF THOMAS NELSON
& ZONDERVAN

WestBow Press books may be ordered through booksellers or by contacting:

WestBow Press
A Division of Thomas Nelson & Zondervan
1663 Liberty Drive
Bloomington, IN 47403
www.westbowpress.com
844-714-3454

ISBN: 979-8-3850-2979-2 (sc)
ISBN: 979-8-3850-2980-8 (e)

Library of Congress Control Number: 2024915103

Print information available on the last page.

WestBow Press rev. date: 8/1/2024

Dedication

I thank my loving family for all their support throughout my life, and I also want to thank everyone who has supported and helped me throughout my incarceration.

In memory of

My heartfelt sorrow and remorse to Mr. Terrance Kurtz, the victim of my crime. I sincerely apologize to his family, the State of Florida, and all people whom I have victimized.

Contents

Chapter One

Home

....

Greetings. My name is James Dean Anderson. I was born on February 20th, 1962, to my parents Ernest and Ruth Holway. Dad was a World War Two, Marine veteran, a big man of Irish and English descent. Mom was Italian and Portuguese, a small woman with a loving heart, a person who was all about the family.

The place of my birth was Cambridge, Massachusetts, just outside of Boston. My parents already had four children when I was born, all girls, starting with Angela, then Sharon, Donna, and Judith. Mom named me after her father, James. But as far back as I can remember, Mom would call me Jim. And whenever I meet somebody new, I invite them to call me by my nickname, Jim.

When I was born my family lived in Maynard, Massachusetts. Shortly thereafter we moved into a fairly new house on 48 Sunshine Drive in Marlboro, Mass. It was a nice red house with a good size yard, and a big hill with woods in the backyard. Without question, 48 Sunshine Drive is the only place I have ever known as, Home.

My home was in a really nice neighborhood that was full of kids. Some were older than me, some were younger, and many were my age. My best friend was a girl named Kathy. She was a tough kid, the person I loved growing up with.

Kathy was my best friend, but my first violent crime was committed against her older brother Kevin. I was only five years old at the time.

1

Kevin was riding by on his bike, and he said something that triggered my anger. I threw a watering can at him and it struck him in the head, causing a gash that needed stitches. This began my list of problems with anger.

Mom was brought up in the Catholic religion. Thus, like other families in the neighborhood, we attended a Catholic church called St. Matthias. The services were the normal Catholic rituals. This was my introduction to the fact that there is an Almighty God, the creator of all things.

In my first two years of schooling, I went to a school across town for kindergarten, and another school further across town for first grade. From there, second grade thru sixth was spent at a new school called The Farm Road School. It was just walking distance from home.

My best memories of 48 Sunshine Drive was Summer time. Just the ability to go outdoors in a tee-shirt and shorts was a wonderful experience. Me and Kathy's friendship song went like this, "We had joy, we had fun, we had seasons in the sun." And the fun would continue on into the night with games such as Hide and Go Seek.

My worst memories of 48 Sunshine Drive was the way my father would express his anger. It would really frighten me, especially if his anger was being manifested towards my mother, or towards me and my sister Judy through beatings. Dad did not have the effective communication skills needed to express his emotion of anger. Unfortunately, I picked up on his negative behavior of uncontrolled anger.

Occasionally, my parents would take us down to Provincetown on the tip of Cape Cod to visit my grandparents on my mother's side, James and Angela Metallo. They lived in a small resort town known for its lobster fishing and street artists. The town was built on the sand dunes of Cape Cod. I would love going to the ocean beach in Provincetown, for the waves were great fun to play in.

Chapter Two

Sports, My Little Helper, The 70s

Sports is a big part of life in the Boston area. As far back as I can remember, Mom was taking me to Fenway Park to watch the Boston Red Sox play baseball, and to the old Boston Garden to watch the Bruins play ice hockey. This began my love for team sports. And when the Boston Patriots (who became the New England Patriots) came into the NFL, Mom would take me to watch them as well.

My father spent a lot of time at work and could not go to the games that Mom was bringing me to watch. But during the Summer, Dad loved to water ski. And at a very young age he taught me how to ski. In my second year of the sport I had become a descent slalom skier.

We had a nice Glastron ski boat. My father named our boat Jimmy Boy, after me, his only son. Our boat had a 115 horsepower Evinrude motor. Jimmy Boy jumped out of the water when Dad would hit full throttle! And as far back as I can remember Dad would tell me, "Jim, this is your boat when you are old enough to take care of it." Our boat was like a second best friend to me. I loved Jimmy Boy.

The lake we skied on in Marlboro was called Fort Meadow. It was actually two lakes connected by a short passageway called The Narrows. Our lake was full of ski boats, especially on the Fourth of July.

Water skiing was a special bond between me and my father. After

3

a long fun day on the lake, me and Dad would go to the Friendly's Ice Cream Shop for some nice cold chocolate frappes (shakes). I loved those times with my father.

Well before I received my driver's license, Dad displayed a great amount of trust in me. At the age of thirteen I became his driver when it was his turn to ski. Yes, early on I learned how to drive, Jimmy Boy.

Earlier in my youth, Mom and me were able to get Dad's permission for me to play ice hockey. I learned to play the game at the age of nine. And when my father saw that I was getting good at the game, he was all in. Dad learned the game and became one of my coaches. He even built me a small ice rink in our side yard.

I was not the biggest player on our team. But I had a lot of speed and a good ability to stick handle the puck. Yes, through hours of practice on our home ice rink, I was able to pattern my game after my first sports hero, Bobby Orr, the Boston Bruins' superstar defenseman.

Sports was a major part of my youth. True enough. But my father also instilled in me something that was very important. A good work ethic. And he started this when I was still a young boy.

Dad worked as a machinist on the weekdays. But on the weekends, he had his own business as a gardener-landscaper. He took care of the property for a rich elderly lady, a widow who lived in the historic small town of Concord, Massachusetts. Her name was Mrs. Powell.

I became Dad's "Little Helper." That is what he would call me. It was my first job, and over the years my father and me took good care of Mrs. Powell's land. This included a lot of grass cutting, raking leaves, especially in the Fall, and weeding her wonderful flower gardens. She was a really nice lady.

During the colder months Dad would store our boat Jimmy Boy in a garage on Mrs. Powell's property. As the warmer weather approached, I remember looking through the garage windows at Jimmy Boy and thinking, It won't be long! And before I knew it, we were back on the water!

Throughout the 60s and 70s my father never changed, for he was as square as you could get, crewcut and all. But during the late 60s and into the 70s, our society was going through a major change, via the hippie era. And Dad could not stop me, as I changed along with America, long hair, bellbottoms and all. Yes, the 1970s transformed our country, including me, my sisters, and the neighborhood.

One thing that did not change from the 60s and into the 70s was the problem I had controlling my emotion of anger. My bad temper would manifest itself from time to time through fits of rage. And one day it almost cost my sister Judy a severe injury.

On a cold winter day, Judy and me were having a bad argument. When the arguing had ended, I headed out back of the house to take out some trash. I was not dressed for the bitter cold weather. And when I walked onto the back porch, Judy slammed the door shut and locked me out. I screamed at her to open the door, but she just stood there at the door window making a face. In a fit of rage, I punched my fist right through the window, shattering the glass into her face. She ran away screaming, sending fear throughout my mind.

I got the door opened and ran in to make sure she was alright. Thankfully, she suffered no injuries, but my arm was cut up pretty bad. We agreed to keep the truth from our father, making up a story that I slipped on the icy porch. Sure glad she kept the truth a secret. But the incident continued my list of problems with anger.

Chapter Three

Jr High, Divorce, Rocky

After grade school I went onto Junior High School, 7th and 8th grade. The school was in the center of Marlboro's Main Street. It was the original Marlboro High School, a three story building. And it was also the background for the night time hang out of Marlboro's older teens. If you needed some marijuana, as Bob Seger's song declared, the pot was Down on Main Street!

I met my first real love in Jr High. Her name was Mary Beth. She was a real tomboy, a tough girl who played ice hockey better than most boys our age. Her slap shot was way better than mine. We stayed together throughout our Jr High days.

Mary Beth got me involved with the Dukes of Marlboro drum and bugle corp. We played the baritone horns in parades and field competitions. The Dukes of Marlboro were a great drum and bugle corp. And my sister Judy also joined the corp with us as a rifle twirler. She was really good at it.

In the mid 70s an event happened that caught me really off guard. My parents got divorced. They were married for over twenty five years. Yes, they had their problems, but I never foresaw the divorce. And I certainly wasn't prepared for it.

My father was the disciplinary figure of our home. But after the divorce he was gone, and I began to go down a dark road of rebellious young teen living. I started hanging out with a kid who was a year older than me named Tommy. We got into shoplifting, stealing items such as candles for our neighborhood fort in the woods, and record albums, especially Rock and Roll music. And I would give some of these albums away to the older teens to be more accepted.

I began to get into the party lifestyle, skipping school, drinking beer and smoking pot. Rock and Roll music was always on in my room. My favorite bands were Boston (naturally), Yes, and, Styx. And my freshman year at Marlboro High School was my worst grade level, including my first "F". Indeed, I had become a Pothead, smoking and selling it. I was arrested twice for possession of marijuana.

My mother had her own problems. She also went down a dark road, alcoholism. Mom stayed in a bar called, Robin's Roost. I hated seeing her in that place.

During the mid 70s a positive influence entered my life. ROCKY. When Sylvester Stallone's movie Rocky came out in 1976, I stayed in the theater for two weeks, watching the early and late shows over and over again, and many times thereafter. I loved the Rocky character. He became the big brother figure that I never had. And I wanted to be just like him, especially when it came to working out. Yes, my exercise program went to a whole new level. I idolized, Rocky.

The Rocky character instilled in me a dream. I did not have the size to become a pro hockey player, so I started putting more effort into water skiing. And with some talk of water skiing being allowed into the Summer Olympics, I began to train really hard to become proficient at slalom water skiing. My goal was to turn pro. It would be a real life Rocky story of the northern skier making it big in the southern dominated sport of water skiing.

A stunt I tried in school did not help the goal. It was my freshman year in High School. The stunt was to walk on the top of the guard railings of a wheelchair ramp. But I slipped and fell off, going head first to the floor. The concussion was so severe that I developed a seizure disorder and was placed on medication. This furthered my decline in school.

Chapter Four

Scratch, Homeless, Grudge

My mother and father both got remarried. Dad married a woman named Jeanne. Mom wedded a man she met at the bar named Whit. He could never become the disciplinary figure I lost with my father.

Mom decided to sell our house on 48 Sunshine Drive. We moved into a condominium in an apartment development called Windsor Heights. It was a nice place, but it was not home. And soon thereafter, Mom and Whit got divorced, and we move again into a small apartment.

I tried living with Dad and Jeanne in their house, but that didn't work out. My father found some pot in my room, and he sent me back to my mother. But she had married another drunk named Bob. And one night when he tried to bully me, I beat him up really bad.

Mom could see that I was going down a long dark road. I was a young man which was full of anger. And she would often tell me, "Jim, you need to give your life to the Lord!" But at the time my mind was set on one thing, survival.

My mother called Dad for some help with me. They did not know it, but I was listening on another phone. She was pleading with him for help. I cannot forget his reply. My father said, "He's going to have to scratch." In other words, he did not want to be bothered with me. And when he said that, I jumped into their conversation and asked, "Scratch?"

I could not live with my father, and I couldn't live with Mom and her drunk husband. Thus, I packed up some clothes in a suitcase, and found a place on the side of Route 20 in some bushes to sleep. I had become homeless.

I remembered that the Windsor Heights condominiums had storage shacks, one for each condo. So, I found an empty condo and used its storage shack for better shelter. It was about six feet long, four feet high, and four feet wide. It was a little larger than a casket.

During my time in the shack I felt overwhelmed with anger and grief. I could not believe my life had gone downhill so fast. Just a year or so before the shack I was at home on 48 Sunshine Drive. Now I was homeless. And this began a very strong grudge of anger towards my father. I just couldn't believe that he did not care about my situation, "Scratch!" He was at his nice home. I was homeless, living in a shack, crying myself to sleep.

Chapter Five

Work, Jimmy Boy, Rage

Thankfully, my sister Donna helped me get out of the shack. She found me a place to stay with a friend of hers named Diane. And it was good timing, for the cold weather was moving into the Boston area.

There was no way I could graduate on time from High School with my Class of 1980. I tried to join the Army, but was rejected because of my seizure disorder. So I entered the workforce.

At the age of seventeen I got a job at a wire goods factory in the center of Marlboro. They produced wire racks for items such as books and magazines. My job on the assembly line was machine spot welding. It was real boring work. And my coworkers treated me as an unwanted outsider, a person who was too young to be there. They did not know the whole story of, "Scratch."

I left the wire goods factory for a job at a boot factory in Marlboro called, Frye Boots. They produced cowboy style boots. It was another boring assembly line job. And once again I was treated as a strange outsider, someone too young to be working there. But I had to scratch out a living and find my own place to live.

My homeless situation began a strong grudge of anger towards my father. True enough. But at least we had our boat Jimmy Boy to keep a tie between us. Unfortunately, he tore that tie to pieces!

I purchased an AMC Spirit car for three thousand dollars. It turned out to be a real lemon, a junk car which was running me into debt. So,

I got rid of it by smashing it into a tree to get the insurance money of three grand. And I used the money to pay off the loan, get out of debt, and buy another cheap car.

A couple weeks after getting out of debt my father called me over to his home. He offered to sell me our boat Jimmy Boy. I was absolutely shocked! His offer caught me so off guard. And the price? Three thousand dollars, the same amount of money that I had risked serious injury to get out of debt by crashing that car into a tree. I walked out, shaking my head in disbelief, and leaving him without an answer.

After a week my father called me with the same proposition. My answer? "NO!" I was not buying our boat he had promised was mine! A couple of days later I went by his house. Jimmy Boy was gone. And that was the last straw. My grudge of anger was sealed!

My birth name was James Ernest Holway. James, after my mother's father's name, and Ernest Holway after my father's name. Thus, James Ernest Holway.

When Dad sold our boat Jimmy Boy, I wanted him completely out of my life, including his part of my name. So I began to search through a phone book for a new last name. I narrowed it down to three, then two, and finally settled on one, Anderson. And I chose Dean to replace Ernest, my middle name. Thus, I went to the Marlboro Courthouse and legally changed my name to, James Dean Anderson. In my mind, my father was gone for good!

The grudge I held towards my father made my problems with anger much worse. I was committing "road rage" incidents before road rage was even used as a term. And I committed acts of vengeance that were no doubt crimes, such as damaging people's property, as well as their vehicles, and physically hurting people. And a common theme emerged, problems with coworkers. I could not live at peace in society, for I had a compulsive behavior addiction of uncontrolled anger.

Chapter Six

The Rambo Influence

Sylvester Stallone came out with Rocky Two, and Rocky Three (The Eye of the Tiger). These movies inspired me to keep my dream alive of becoming a pro water skier. I would practice really hard on the Fort Meadow Ski Club's slalom course to keep that Rocky dream alive.

The Rocky character was a great inspiration to me. But in 1982, a new influence entered into my life. And unlike the positive influence of Rocky, this new influence would become very negative.

I began to see commercial previews of a movie Sylvester Stallone had made, a movie with a whole new character. The movie was entitled, First Blood. And the name of Stallone's new character was, John Rambo.

Sylvester Stallone's Rocky character was a real life person to me. I could not imagine Stallone as any other character, for in my mind it would not be real. So the movie previews of First Blood did not catch my attention. That all changed when I went to see the movie. First Blood caught more than my attention. Rambo became a second older brother figure to me, another character for me to idolize.

Like the movie Rocky, I went to see the first Rambo movie over and over again in the theater, and several times thereafter on cable television. And like Rocky, I wanted to be just like my new hero, John Rambo, including going out into the woods with my big knife practicing survival skills.

The Rocky character was based on a man who had a loving heart, a person who overcame the odds. Rambo was the complete opposite. The character of John Rambo was based on anger, rebellion, and vengeance through violence.

I was fertile ground to take in the negative influence of Rambo. He was an Army Green Beret, Vietnam Veteran. When I was in elementary school, we sang a song about the Army Green Berets. So Rambo, a Green Beret war hero, automatically caught my attention. Yes, it was easy for me to relate with John Rambo, for we had certain things in common. I had been homeless and was a loner. Rambo was homeless and was a loner. I was a grudge holder, a man full of anger towards my father. Rambo was a grudge holder, a man full of anger towards American civilians who protested against him. And neither one of us could seem to fit in with society.

The choice I made to idolize the John Rambo character was a terrible decision. My behavior was already very negative. The Rambo influence took my mind from a bad state to worse. And over time, my behavior went from dangerous to deadly. Indeed, the writing on the wall of my back was clear, for it read, Bound for State Prison. I did not know the writing was there, but my mother did, as she continued to plead with me to give my life to the Lord.

Chapter Seven

Laura, The Move

In the early 80s I had two girlfriends, Sharon and Laura. I felt the need to settle down with one of them. Sharon was not ready for the married life. But Laura was, so we had a private ceremony and became married. And I will give Laura a great deal of credit, for she knew the kind of man she was marrying, a man with a severe problem with anger.

I still loved the winter sport of ice hockey. So I joined an adult hockey league. Laura was my biggest fan. But unfortunately, one night she had to witness one of my savage fits of rage.

During one of my hockey games a player on another team felt led to annoy me with some cheap shots, hoping to get me off my game. He succeeded. For after he gave me a good punch to my chest, I stopped short and swung my stick at him, slashing him in the side of his neck with the blade of my stick. I cussed him out as he rolled on the ice in extreme pain. The officials ejected me from the game, but no doubt it was another non-prosecuted crime that involved my anger. And on our way to the apartment I had no words for Laura.

I still wanted to take a shot at becoming a professional water skier. This would mean moving down to Florida where I could train year round. Mom was against the idea of me leaving the family in Massachusetts. But, as one of my biggest fans, she gave me her support.

My mother had an old friend who told her about a trailer that was for sale in Florida. So Laura and Mom went to Lakeland, Florida to check out the trailer. Mom went ahead and purchased it, which opened the door for me to move into the Sunshine State of Florida.

The plan was simple. Me and Laura would live in the trailer, taking care of it till my mother was ready to use it as a winter retirement home. And this would give me a chance to chase my Rocky dream of becoming a professional water skier.

The trailer was in an elderly retirement development in central Lakeland. It was a nice two bedroom, two bath trailer. And the agreement we made with the trailer park management was clear. Me and Laura would live in the park, taking care of my mother's trailer, but we had to keep our noise level down in the elderly development. We signed the agreement and the move was sealed.

The first year in Florida went as planned. I found a good water ski club that had a nice slalom course for me to train on. And when I was not working at a van conversion company, I was doing a large amount of cross training of weightlifting and jogging. But then something happened that caught me really off guard.

I never physically abused my wife Laura. But without question, my problems with anger had scarred her emotionally. And when she could no longer handle it, she left and divorced me. Once again, I was an angry loner.

Chapter Eight

Hungry Howies, Terry

....

My life went on after Laura. But one thing stayed the same, my usual problems with a coworker. The manager at the van conversion company where I worked created a problem. We ended up getting into a heated argument, which escalated into a physical confrontation. Thus, I lost another job and moved onto the next one.

I was hired as a delivery driver for a Hungry Howies Pizza store in the south side of Lakeland. The job was working out well at first. The work kept me off my feet, leaving me plenty of energy to workout and water ski. It also paid fairly well. I was even able to acquire a new pickup truck.

I worked at the Hungry Howies store for over two years, becoming the shop's Delivery Coordinator. I would come off a delivery, set up some pizza orders for the other drivers, and go back on the road. It was a pretty good job.

The job at the store was on the night shift. When I finished my work and went to the trailer, I would stay up late doing my usual, watching movies that glorified criminal gun violence. Movies, such as the Death Wish series with Charles Bronson, Taxi Driver with Robert DeNiro, and of course, First Blood, the first Rambo movie with Stallone were always on my television. I did not know it at the time, but I had chosen a lifestyle that over the years desensitized my mind to how precious human life really is.

I saw an article in a Muscle and Fitness magazine about the gym where Sylvester Stallone worked out at. I wrote Stallone a letter, thanking him for influencing my life, and sent it off to his gym. I couple of months later I received a good size envelope from Hollywood, California. No name, just the address. I opened it and took out a photo of Rambo with Sylvester Stallone's autograph on it in blue ink. There was no letter, just the autographed picture. I framed it and put it on my nightstand.

Just like Rambo, I always had a knife on me. But something happened that led me to buy some firearms. I was robbed at gunpoint. So, I went to a store in the south side of Lakeland called Guns Galore, and I purchased a 32 caliber automatic handgun and a 38 special Taurus revolver. The person who had a major problem controlling his anger, Jim, was now further armed and much more dangerous in free society.

About a year into my work at Hungry Howies, a young man applied for a job at our store. His name was Terrance Kurtz, but went by the name, Terry. I trained him as one of our drivers, and Terry became very good at delivering. We worked together for about a year. Then, it ended in tragedy.

Chapter Nine

Failure, Faith, Fear

My Rocky dream of becoming a professional water skier came to an end. I was a very good skier, but not good enough to turn pro. And when the dream crashed in failure, I was faced with yet another painful experience in my life.

Despite the failure of my dream, I had to move on with life. As I continued my work at the store, I tried to come up with a plan for some type of career. I decided to go into truck driving and began to study the work.

One day I was informed that my coworker Terry had fallen on hard times and was homeless, living out of his truck. Knowing how it felt to be homeless, I offered him a place to stay with me in the trailer until he could get back on his feet. And I made it very clear to Terry, that park management would not tolerate any loud noise. He agreed and moved in.

A couple of weeks after Terry moved in I was called to the trailer park manager's office. He informed me that Terry was blasting the stereo when I was not there, and that our neighbors were complaining. The manager gave me this option, either I tell Terry to leave the trailer or he would have us both removed. Thus, I had no choice, I had to tell Terry to leave.

Terry had been promoted to a co-manager's job at the store. He was one of the overseers of my work. After I removed Terry from the trailer he began to make my job really difficult. The old curse was back, a problem with a coworker. And it began to fill my mind with stress.

During this time of struggling with Terry, a young woman came into our store and we started having a conversation. Her name was Kathy. She was in Florida on a college vacation visiting her family. Kathy invited me to a church service at the Family Worship Center in Lakeland.

God had an interesting way to call me to a church service. He sent a pretty young lady named Kathy, my childhood best friend's name, and had her invite me to church. Without a second thought I accepted her invitation.

I attended many Catholic services growing up in Massachusetts. The service Kathy brought me to was completely different. It was an auditorium setting with a stage full of flowers, and a pastor preaching from the Bible like I never heard before. This was all new to me.

When the service was about over the preacher invited anyone to the front who wanted to accept Jesus Christ as their personal Lord and Savior. Some people went to the front to receive salvation. After they prayed the service ended. Then me and Kathy went out for a nice meal, and we parted ways.

The church service Kathy brought me to was on a Wednesday night. As the next Wednesday approached I felt called to go back to the next service. When the alter call was made I went to the front to accept Jesus Christ as my Lord and Savior.

The situation with Terry started getting worse and worse. So I increased my efforts to leave the store and go into truck driving. But it would take some time for me to get my truck driver's license and get a new job. I related this to Terry, even offering him a handshake for peace. He would not accept it and kept on pushing me out of my job.

I began to have an overwhelming fear that something horrible was about to happen in my life. There was no question about it, I could sense that danger was just around the corner. And the fear was so strong that it began to trigger mild seizure activity from the head injury I had as a child.

The seizures became an attack on my mind. During the mild

seizures my eyes would close, and I could see an image of a man in my mind as he walked by in front of me. I could not completely see his face, for he had a cape on with a high collar. And every seizure he kept asking me the same question, "Do you want this life or the one I have to offer you?"

I brought all this information to my doctor. He began to increase my medication. And if that did not help, his plan was to have me evaluated by a psychiatrist or psychologist to try and find out where all the fear was coming from. It was a good plan, but I needed far more help than that. I needed help from the one who gave me life to begin with, Almighty God!

I needed God's help, but I did not know how to pray. I didn't know how to ask Almighty God for help. So this is what I did. I took out the old family Bible I had saved throughout the years and put it on my bed. It was a big ole Catholic Bible. And I remember looking at it and thinking, I sure hope this book can teach me how to pray.

I opened the Bible right in the middle. What I found was Psalm 140. Yes, Psalm 140. The message of the Psalm can be summed up in this sentence; Deliver me oh Lord from the trap that has been set for me. And I began to use this Psalm as my prayer for help. Deliver me oh Lord from, the trap!

All these events were happening in the Summer of 1989, failure, faith, and fear. I even slipped into a state of paranoia. Every time I came into the trailer at night my 38 special revolver was in my hand, and I would search out the whole trailer, making sure no one was in there. I kept that gun close to me at all times. And I continued to fill my mind with the wine of violence through movies. My favorite drink? First Blood, the first Rambo movie.

Chapter Ten

The Crime, The Drive

The night of August 16th, 1989 began as normal. I would be the driver to start off the night shift, and the driver to finish it. The manager was off and Terry was in charge of the store.

When a driver would finish his shift, it was his duty to pitch in on the clean up of pots and pans. As the night went on I began to notice something strange. After Terry would cash out a driver, he would not give them any clean up duty. Thus, the pots and pans began to pile up in the sink area. And I had an uneasy feeling that Terry was going to dump all the clean up on me.

The night came to a finish, and me and Terry were the only ones in the store. When he cashed me out, I asked him what he wanted me to do for clean up. Terry pointed to the sink area, which was loaded with pots, pans and so forth. I said, "I will do half with you and we will get it done together." He said it was all on me. I gave Terry the same offer, but he refused. I clocked out and left the store.

That night I could not get to sleep. Once again, I was overwhelmed with fear. So, I went to the store to check on it. The clean up was done, but I noticed a problem with the delivery paperwork. I took it with me to the trailer.

When I went into work the next day my weekly time card was gone. So I punched in a blank card. Then I made a phone call to the store manager, asking him to come in for a meeting between me, him, and Terry. I was in desperate need of some help.

The manager came in for the meeting, but it turned into a heated argument between me and Terry. I gave the manager my two weeks notice of ending my employment and left on a delivery. My level of anger was in the very high range.

Upon my arrival back to the store, me and Terry got into a confrontation, which escalated into violence. After I committed this horrible crime I fled the scene. The fit of rage in which I had entered into was so strong, that when I left the scene I could not remember what I had done. It was all blacked out. And after my anger subsided, I chose to flee the state of Florida.

On that same day, August 17th, 1989, my doctor wrote a message in my medical file concerning his plan. It read as follows; "8-17-89 Tried to reach patient. No answer."

I drove all night and into the next day. When I got up into South Carolina I stopped at a phone booth to call my mother in Massachusetts. It was the phone call she always feared.

Mom knew instantly that something was wrong. She began to ask, "Jim, what happened? Jim, what happened?" I remember telling her, "They kept on pushing." Then she asked, "Jim, what did you do?" I said, "I don't know." Thus, I instructed her to have my sister Donna, a police officer up in Massachusetts, to call the police in Lakeland and find out what I had done. Then I told her I would call Donna when I got up into North Carolina. We hung up and I got back onto the highway.

When I got into Fayetteville, North Carolina I stopped to call my sister Donna. She informed me that I had shot one of my coworkers to death, and that I was wanted for First Degree Murder. I was absolutely devastated! For I could not comprehend how I had committed such a violent act, but couldn't remember doing it. My mind was filled with confusion.

Donna advised me to turn myself in to the local authorities. She told me that I should go back to Florida and face the charge through a trial. I agreed, said a goodbye, and hung up the phone.

I went to a small police station there in Fayetteville, North Carolina. After entering the station, I told the officers my name, and that I was wanted for First Degree Murder in Florida. And I told them the gun was in my truck, and gave them the keys. The drive had ended.

Chapter Eleven

The Trial, Prison

After three days in North Carolina, two Polk County detectives brought me back to Florida. I knew one of them, Detective Zarbo. He used my vehicle to try and catch a robber of our delivery drivers. And shortly after getting back into Florida they brought me to the Polk County Jail.

My mother hired a lawyer for me named Jack Edmunds. His son was the first person from their office to interview me. From there, I was visited by a private investigator from Mr. Edmunds' office. And finally, the day before the trial, Jack Edmunds came to see me.

Six months after the crime my trial began. It was a very short trial, only a day and a half long. I was the only person my lawyer called for the defense. My mother and Terry's mother sat together. And when the trial was over, I was found guilty of First Degree Murder, and sentenced to Life in prison, with a minimum mandatory twenty five years in State Prison before becoming eligible for release on parole.

My trial did not go as I hoped. For whatever reason, Mr. Edmunds was not fully informed of what actually happened at the crime scene. There was much more that could have been presented to the jury. But I want to make the following completely clear.

I take full responsibility for the death of my victim, Mr. Terrance Kurtz. If I had left the store while I still had a chance the confrontation would not have escalated into an unjustifiable homicide. I put myself in a position to where my anger reached the highest level known to mankind, an insane blackout fit of rage. And when it was over, Terry was not spared from my compulsive behavior addiction to anger.

Shortly after the trial I was transferred to the Florida Department of Corrections, Central Florida Reception Center Prison. When I arrived there, I was in a depressed state of shock and spent a week in the infirmary. But when I was released onto the compound something miraculous happened. The small mustard seed of faith that was planted in me at The Family Worship Center in Lakeland, that began to take root through my Psalm 140 prayer, started to grow. And here is how that happened.

One morning at the Reception Center prison a call went out over the dorm loudspeaker, "Morning Devotion Service, check out." I felt totally led in my heart to go. It was a small service led by a nice volunteer named Reverend Morton. We prayed, sang a song, read the Our Daily Bread devotional and prayed out. Reverend Morton gave me my first personal Bible. Every weekday I went to his morning devotional service.

For the first time in my life I began to read the Bible, God's word. I started in the New Testament, namely the Gospels, and went forward from there. I was also reading the book of Proverbs. I found it amazing at how much the Bible spoke about the dangers of anger. And without question, the key to overcoming problems with anger was summed up in one word, forgiveness.

Through the Morning Devotion Services and reading God's word, I received a very clear message. I had to completely forgive my father and release that old grudge of anger. And when I released all that unforgiveness, God granted me, Victory over Anger!

Almighty God created in me a clean heart and renewed in me a right spirit that was based on love, forgiveness, and mercy. Indeed, the Lord removed the Rambo influence of anger, rebellion, and vengeance through violence from my mind. My days of being an angry violent person were over!

I wrote Dad a letter of gratitude, thanking him for all the good things he had done in my life. Releasing the grudge of anger allowed me to do this. And through God's grace, my relationship with my father was healed.

Chapter Twelve

Union, Mom's Move

In April of 1990 I was transferred to Union Correctional Institution, a maximum security prison in the city of Raiford. When the Blue Bird bus pulled up to the prison I got my first look at "The Rock," the original Florida State Prison. The building was a three story high huge square. And I remember saying to myself, "Man, I bet that old place gets cold!" I do not like cold temperatures. But thankfully it was closed down and I was housed in a regular dorm.

Within my first month at Union I received my GED, and then I entered the Vocational Welding class. I learned how to arc (stick) weld pretty fast. Then I began to teach the other inmates how to weld. When my free world supervisor observed me instructing inmates in welding, he put me in charge of the arc section of the class.

One day while I was straightening out the arc area of the shop, I found a knife. Not a shank, like it is called in prison. No, this was an Army style knife that had been left behind. Rambo would have loved this knife. I could've gotten it back to the dorm, but I ignored the temptation and gave it to my supervisor to be destroyed.

Early on at Union I was able to avoid any real serious problems with other inmates. I became a respected participant at our All Souls Chapel, the place of my baptism. The Friday night services and the Sunday morning services were my favorites. I also listened to good Bible studies on my radio, and I received a good understanding of end-time prophesy.

In October of 1990 I was called to the Chapel. Chaplain McCullom informed me that I was selected to attend a Kairos weekend. I asked him, "What is Kairos?" He asked me if I had signed up for the Kairos weekend, and I said no. So he called in the head chaplain. He informed Chaplain Cornett that I was on the Kairos list, but had not signed up for it. Chaplain Cornett looked at my name, and said that Reverend Morton from the Orlando reception prison called him and requested that I be put through the Kairos weekend. Thus, I attended Kairos 29 and sat at the table of St. Paul. It was a wonderful weekend, full of love and fellowship. And to my surprise, Reverend Morton came to our closing ceremony. It was great to see him again.

The dorm I was assigned to became a no smoking building. Many of my brothers in Christ began to move into the dorm. We started a Bible study in my cell. Each of us would take turns giving a message from God's word. This became my foundation of giving speeches.

My recreation time at Union consisted of weightlifting, jogging, and playing the sport of handball. I over did it on the weight pile and herniated the last spinal disc in my lower back. It was a very painful injury. Later on in 2007 the disc had to be surgically removed, and that area of my lower spine was fused to my tailbone.

In 1996 my mother Ruth did something that was an amazing act of love. Mom left our entire family up in Massachusetts to move down here to Florida. And she made the move for one reason, so she could visit her son in prison. Mom was sixty eight years old when she made the move.

An old friend of my mother helped her to find a nice place to live in Daytona Beach. Twice a month she would make the long drive up to Raiford to visit me. And if other family members would come down here from Massachusetts, she would take them to Union as well. Also, my father and step-mother Jeanne would come down for visits.

I spent a total of five years working in Union's vocational welding shop. When the prison closed down the class, I received a job at the PRIDE Broom Plant. I made the maximum fifty five cents an hour. Our shop was inside the PRIDE Tag (license plate) Plant. And I worked in the Broom Plant for five years, becoming the Leadman of the shop.

During my first seven years at Union I was on fire for God. I believed he had a plan to get me out of prison through the appeal process. In 1997 that belief came to a screeching halt, when I received a final notice from the appellate court that was very clear; Mr. Anderson, No more appeals! And my Life sentence began to really kick in. I had eighteen more years to do in prison before becoming illegible for parole.

My mindset towards God became very negative. I believed he had let me down, and that I was going to remain in prison for the rest of my life. I stopped praying, fellowshipping, and going to chapel services. God's response? The rod of chastisement. An inmate in the dorm disrespected me in my cell. A confrontation occurred, and I was sent to confinement with my first Disciplinary Report. The prison administration sentenced me to sixty days in confinement. I was in a state of pure misery.

During my time of rebellion, I never stopped reading my Bible. The Chapel would also send me material to read in confinement. Through my readings I kept getting the same message over and over again. I had given my life to the Lord and was his servant. God was on the throne of my life, not me. I was bought with a great price, and if it was his will for me to remain in prison to do his work, then his will be done, not mine!

On the twenty third day of the sixty days confinement sentence, I repented. I fell down to me knees crying, and asked Almighty God to forgive me. My heart became filled with joy, as I began to dance around the confinement cell praising the Lord! On that same day in which I repented, a call came over the cell intercom, "Anderson, pack your stuff, you're going back to the compound." It was like hearing the voice of God himself. And I have never looked back, remaining Disciplinary Report free for all these years. Praise God!

Chapter Thirteen

Tomoka, Horizon

NASCAR races were a southern sport. I used to love watching the races as a child in Massachusetts on ABC's Wide World of Sports, especially the Daytona 500. Cale Yarborough was my first favorite driver. But in the early 80s when Dale Earnhardt came along, he became my favorite. I loved his tough aggressive style of racing. Dale was like an ice hockey player on a racetrack. And I got to see him race in person when I went to the 1989 Daytona 500, six months before my case happened.

Mom lived right down the road from the track in Daytona Beach. I would encourage her to go check out a race, but she would say, "Jim, I'm not interested in racing." One day she said to me over the phone, "Jim, guess where I'm going Sunday?" Her church was running a food stand at the track, and she went to her first Daytona 500. And that was all it took. Mom became a big Dale Earnhardt fan!

Tomoka Correctional Institution was in Daytona Beach, about fifteen minutes from where my mother lived. She began to inform me that Tomoka C I was a descent prison. For she was a Kairos volunteer at the camp. And I started giving some serious consideration of leaving Union for Tomoka.

In October of 1999, me and Mom had another great visit. After she left, I gave her the normal three hours to get home before calling to make sure she made it home safely. She was seventy one years old at the time.

When I called my mother, she was not at home. So I gave her fifteen more minutes and tried again, but still there was no answer. When she finally answered, I asked, "Mom, what took you so long to get home?" She said, "I got tired after leaving the prison and pulled over to take a nap." The place where she pulled into was a cemetery. My mother was sleeping in a graveyard. I immediately put in for a meeting with my Classification Officer and requested a transfer to Tomoka Correctional Institution. Within two weeks I was transferred to Tomoka C I. And this made it much easier for Mom to visit me.

When I arrived at Tomoka I was totally shocked. Union was very strict when it came to inmate compound movement. Tomoka was the total opposite. The dorms were open before the 8 AM shift came on duty. I could walk right out the door to the compound in my tee-shirt and shorts, headphones on, listening to my radio. The recreation yard was not in one spot, but spread out over the prison grounds. Trees were everywhere, and they had park style benches all around them. It felt like I landed on a college campus.

Tomoka C I had a new faith based dorm program called, Horizon. It was in operation for three months before I arrived. The Horizon program was on the side one of F Dorm. And one thing was for certain, I wanted in that program. For God's hand was at work in Horizon.

The Horizon program was twelve months long. When the first six months were near completion, side two of F Dorm was going Horizon as well. So I signed up for the program. I believed that this was God's plan for me. But when the list came out for the participants of Horizon Two, I was not on it, and I became very disappointed. Then something interesting happened.

I was going down the walkway towards the Horizon dorm, and I was thinking about how much I wanted to be in that program. As I looked at the dorm a tall man came out of side two and he started walking in my direction. The first thing I noticed about him was his new prison uniform, all creased up and looking sharp. When he got closer to me he asked, "James, have you been selected for Horizon?" My first thought was, How does this inmate know my name when I've never seen him before? I said, "No, I'm not on the list." As he passed by he looked down at me and said, "It will not be long." His words lifted my spirit.

The following day I was doing some landscaping work around the Chapel. One of the orderlies came out and asked, "James, there is an opening in side one of the Horizon program, would you like to fill the spot?" Heck Yeah! So I was moved into Horizon. And later that day I tried to find the tall man on side two of our dorm. I wanted to thank him for his word of encouragement, but I couldn't find him. In fact, I never saw him again! And I am good with faces. An angel?

After my first six months in Horizon, the original participants were about to graduate and go back onto the compound. Having been in the program as a fill in, I was selected to the new group of Horizon participants. It was called, Horizon Three.

The Horizon year starts off with a Kairos weekend. Thus, I was blessed to go through a second Kairos. Our family name was St. Timothy. And after our year ended, I was asked to stay in the program as an Alumni. A few months later I became an Encourager (family leader). I also became the program Grandfather, and finally the Clerk (program leader). In total, I spent seven years in the Horizon program.

While in Horizon I worked on a very important project. Each month some youthful offenders were court ordered to come into Tomoka to hear me and some of the other community members give speeches about crime and incarceration. I would give the 10 20 Life video presentation, and then give them a speech which was strictly about gun violence. When I finished my speech, I would always tell them, "You are about to leave this compound and hear a talk from a little old lady who has a son in prison. Make sure you give her a big hug for me, for she is my mother." And they would always do that for me.

The Horizon program had access to videos from the Chapel, such as preaching and teaching videos, good Christian movies, worship music videos, and documentaries. I loved watching these videos. And there was one documentary that really caught my attention. The documentary was entitled, Fatal Addiction. It was about a man named, Ted Bundy.

The day before Ted Bundy was executed in the Florida State Prison electric chair, he gave an interview with Christian psychologist, Dr.

James Dobson. Bundy wanted to get out a message of how the negative influence of pornography led him down the road to violent crime. Porn, namely violent video pornography, became an addiction to him, an addiction that would become deadly.

One may question the motives of why Ted Bundy gave the interview. I totally understand the concern. But, after watching the documentary, I was able to receive a message that was a new revelation to me. What a person watches on a screen, and takes it into their mind, can influence that person in a very negative way.

Dr. Dobson's video convinced me to do a sincere moral inventory of my life prior to incarceration. For I wanted to know if there was anything I was watching in my past which influenced me in a negative way. Indeed, I wanted to know if there was something I had taken into my mind that contributed to my criminal behavior.

The results of my moral inventory were answered really fast. I remembered a question from the State's prosecutor when I was on the stand at my trial. He asked me, "Why do you have a framed picture of Rambo?" I am sure that I gave him the answer in which he wanted the jury to hear, for I said, "He's my idol." The state of Florida was aware of my negative influence well before I was aware of it.

Years before viewing the Fatal Addiction video, I had repented from watching movies that glorified criminal gun violence. God had renewed my mind from the attraction of watching violent movies. But after my moral inventory in Horizon, I was giving a full understanding of the power of influence. Indeed, the negative influence I willingly accepted from that first Rambo movie, First Blood, as well as other criminal gun violence movies, played a part in me going down the road to gun violence. Accepting that negative influence was the worst decision I ever made in my life. And the only person I can blame for making such a bad decision is me, James Dean Anderson.

As for my recreation time at Tomoka, it consisted of weightlifting, handball, and softball. The handball courts at Union were single wall, but the courts at Tomoka were big three wall courts. This was a much bigger challenge, especially in the hot Summer weather.

My visits with Mom were great. I would come into the Visiting

Park, and she would already have a place prepared for us. Mom made sure we had two Bibles, a deck of cards, and a Scrabble game. We started off with prayer and a reading from God's word. Then Mom would say, "Alright, let's play!" She loved playing card games and Scrabble. And in fun we would sell out to each other, talking some good smack.

When my mother was winning a game, one of her favorite lines would be, "How do you like them apples?" If I was winning, one of my lines would be, "Mom, this is a man's prison, and you're going to have to take this whooping like a man!" To that she would reply, "Shut up! I don't want to hear that!" She was a small woman, but a huge competitor.

During one of our visits, it was clear that my mother was going to win the Scrabble game. And I said to her, "Well Mom, it looks like you got this one." To that she replied, "Jim, this is a man's prison, and you're going to have to take this whooping like a man!" She used my line! So I asked her, "Oh, really?" Then she repeated my line again, but much louder. People in the Park started looking at her. So I said, "Mom, hold it down!" But she repeated the line again, this time loud enough for everyone to hear. The Visiting Park got quiet, as everyone looked at her. I was stunned and without words. Mom began to fix her letters, tilting her head a little, ignoring the quiet. Then she looked up at me, and her face said it all, "I don't care what they think about me!" In that moment she was not just my mother, but she was like the little brat sister that I never had. It was a moment I'll always cherish.

Over the years Tomoka became a control movement camp. This made it difficult to do the simple things, like getting some good recreation or just going to the canteen store. In fact, trying to get some shopping done at the canteen was nearly impossible. And I only shopped once a week. So, I put in for a canteen job with Classification. At least then I could make it to the store. I was hired and worked a canteen on the south end of the compound for my last five years at Tomoka.

Chapter Fourteen

The Parole Process

In 2013 a significant event transpired. My mother was having trouble driving and had a car accident. She was eighty five years old at the time. So she had to stop driving, which put an end to our visits. No more would I walk out of the Visiting Park and see her waiting outside the fences to wave goodbye to me. It was heartbreaking not to have her visits.

There was no longer a reason for Mom to stay here in Florida, so she moved back to Massachusetts to be with my sisters. Thus, from 1996 to 2013, seventeen years, Mom lived down here alone in Florida. And as I wrote earlier, she did it for one reason, so she could visit her son in prison, so her son could have a connection to family. What an act of love. What an incredible act of God's love. She fulfilled God's word, "When I was in prison you visited me."

In 2014 my mandatory twenty five years would be complete, making me eligible for parole. So in 2013 I had my Initial Parole Hearing, where the Florida Commission on Offender Review (the parole board), would set my Presumptive Parole Release Date (PPRD). The Commission gave me favor, setting my PPRD at September 21st, 2014, right at the end of my mandatory twenty five years. Thus, I was set for my first Effective Parole Hearing.

I met Ken Cooper at my Kairos weekend in 1990 at Union C I. He was an inmate there at Union, who later became a Kairos volunteer.

We kept in touch during my mandatory twenty five years. And as the director of a transition halfway house in Jacksonville, Ken became my first parole sponsor.

My mother came down from Mass to attend my first Effective Parole Hearing. She went with Ken Cooper. The Commission decided to set off my parole date for two years, with a recommendation to Wakulla Correctional Institution for program participation. Mom was very upset, but Ken told us it was good news for someone with a case such as mine to be put off only two years at their first hearing. And the Commission referred me to a program camp, which displayed a willingness to work with me.

I was not excited about going to Wakulla C I, for it was in the panhandle of Florida. Stories about camps up there were always negative. And the winters would be much colder. I mentioned my feelings about cold temperatures. But I had to go, for it would put me in "the loop," the Commission's parole process. So in September of 2014, I was transferred to Wakulla Correctional Institution.

In August of 2016, I was set for my second Effective Parole Hearing. Mom and Ken Cooper once again went to the hearing together. The Commission chose again to set my date off two years, with a referral to Sumter Correctional Institution's Lifers Program. It was another set off, but Ken continued to encourage us, stating that the Commission was viewing me closely as a good candidate for parole. Thus, I was transferred to Sumter C I, which is near the city of Tampa.

The Lifers Program at Sumter was far more focused on parole than the program at Wakulla. For the classes at Wakulla C I were not for all inmates who were parole eligible. But Sumter's Lifers Program knew they were working with men who had done thirty, forty, some even fifty years in prison. These inmates needed some serious deprisonization.

I became actively involved in the Sumter recreational yard church ministry. Every Thursday we would have a service under a pavilion on the rec yard, and I would give a message once a month. One of my speeches was entitled, The Answer. I later gave it the title, The Power of Influence. More on that speech later in this book.

Me and my father always kept in touch over the years through letters. My step-mother Jeanne had passed away, and Dad, who was now into his nineties, could no longer make the long trip to Florida to visit me. Thankfully, my father became a strong man of faith. And he loved to read my messages about God's word.

While I was at Sumter C I a new "lifers" program was opened up at New River Correctional Institution. About a year into Sumter's two year program, I received a notice from the Commission that they had referred me to the new Pathways Program at New River C I. And when my next Effective Parole Hearing was approaching, it was apparent to me that my parole date would once again be put off, giving me time to participate in this new lifers program.

About a month before I graduated from Sumter's Lifers Program, the canteen operator in our complex was fired. Classification, for whatever reason, could not find a suitable replacement for the canteen job. So they called me out to see if I would take the job. I explained that I was about to graduate from the program and no doubt be transferred to New River C I. But they needed to get the store opened, so I took the job.

A month after I graduated from Sumter's program I got an order from Security, "Anderson, pack your stuff, you're being transferred." I was put on the bus with the other inmates who were transferring. There was long delay. The back door of the bus was unlocked, and an officer announced, "Anderson, get off the bus and go back to your dorm." Sumter C I changed their mind about transferring me. So I headed back to work at the canteen. When the guys in Complex Three saw me coming back they gave me a standing ovation, for they knew I kept the store opened for them. It was a nice moment of feeling appreciated.

As I expected, my third Effective Parole Hearing brought another set off. So I kept on working the canteen job. It would be two years before I was transferred to New River C I's lifers program.

I received my last visit from my mother while I was at Sumter. My sister Sharon brought her down. She was now into her nineties, but Mom still loved to play card games. Also, while I was at Sumter my father passed away. The last letter I received from Dad was written by a nurse.

This is the letter;

Dear Jim,

I am so glad to have heard from you. Thank you for the picture, and I have it hanging on my wall on the bulletin board. I'm really glad that I have someone who helps me write letters to you. I love getting letters from you. I'm feeling very well. It has been getting cool. I think of you often Jim, and I believe you deserve more out of life. I told the nurse writing this letter that you are a really good guy. I will always believe that. I hope you continue to preach the Bible. It is the one thing that keeps me going, and I know it keeps you going too. I am sure many other people have been benefited from your teachings. If you were here I would not have so much trouble finding the right words to say. I know you are doing what you need to do to improve your life. I'll say goodbye for now. Remember, God loves you and so do I.

Love,
Dad

My sister Judy sent me a picture of Dad shortly after he passed away on his bed. A hat with the name Jesus on it was hanging on a panel of wood near his head. I thank God that my loving father, Ernest Holway, is safely with the Lord. Amen.

While I was at Sumter C I, Tom Brady went to the Tampa Bay Buccaneers. Tom was next in line as my sports hero, after Dale Earnhardt, who was after Bobby Orr. And with Sumter being so close to the Tampa Bay area, I was able to follow his play for the Bucs.

In October of 2020, I was transferred to New River Correctional Institution to participate in the Pathways Program. New River C I was right next door to Union C I. So, I went back to the section of Florida where I had started. And a few months later I got to watch Tom Brady win his seventh Super Bowl. Go Tom!

A couple of weeks after arriving at New River, I joined the Pathways Program's Gavel Club. I continued to sharpen up my public speaking skills. And I also continued to polish up my speech, The Power of Influence.

Our Pathways Pioneers Gavel Club had a small ceremony for the changing of leadership. One of the parole Commissioners, Ms. Coonrod, attended the ceremony. Other dignitaries from the Capital in Tallahassee were with her. I was the Table Topics Master, the member who calls up participants at random to answer a question with a short speech. She probably was not expecting it, but I called Ms. Coonrod up for a question. I asked her, "If you were to retire and go on a trip around the world, where would you go and why would you go there?" Ms. Coonrod took off, explaining why she would go to the country of Italy to search out her ancestors. This was our first in person meeting.

I was in my fifth month of the Pathways Program when I had my fourth Effective Parole Hearing in February of 2021. My parole date was set off three years. The Commission wanted me to finish the Pathways Program, and they also gave me a recommendation to Dr. Regina B. Shearn's Corrections Transition Program (CTP), at Everglades Correctional Institution in Miami.

The Pathways Program leadership put me on the fast track. I completed the two year program in only ten months. Then I was transferred down to Everglades C I in Miami to attend the CTP program.

From 2014 to 2021, I zigzagged the state of Florida in the parole process, "the loop." I went from Tomoka in Daytona Beach to Tallahassee in the panhandle, down to the Tampa Bay area, up to the Jacksonville area, and finally down to Miami. And when I entered Dr. Shearn's CTP program, I became a man going home. For that is our CTP slogan, "Men Going Home!"

Dr. Shearn's Corrections Transition Program is the best prison re-entry program in Florida. Much of the program's success revolves around its affiliation with the Florida International University students.

The program also has an excellent aftercare support network at Noah's House, a multiple transitional housing project in Tampa, as well as the Abe Brown Ministries career placement program.

All the classes and functions we do here in CTP revolve around preparing a man to live life successfully on parole. Dr. Shearn's CTP program does the final work of deprisonization, the transforming of a man's prison thinking, to the mind set of living out in society as a well-mannered gentleman. And this is what makes our program so successful.

I became a certified CTP instructor for our Anger Management Class. This class is an intense study on the emotion of anger and the skills needed to manage anger in the proper way. The only reason why I became qualified to instruct the Anger Management Class is because God had granted me, Victory over Anger!

Our CTP Gavel Club is called Voices of Time. I have given a good number of speeches in our club. Recently I gave my speech, The Power of Influence. This speech clearly explains the dangers of what negative influence can do to a person's mind who becomes overly attracted to graphic criminal gun violence on a screen, be it a theater screen, home television, computer tablet or phone. For as it says in God's word, what a person sows in their mind is what they will reap in life. And the message of the speech clearly explains why our country is experiencing such a large escalation of gun violence. It is a speech that needs to be heard in free society, especially by our youth.

The day of my fifth Effective Parole Hearing is approaching. One member of my parole team will not be participating in the hearing, my loving mother, Ruth. In December of 2022, Mom went home to be with the Lord. She passed away peacefully at the age of ninety four.

Mom will not be here to see me living life successfully on parole. But I believe she became a woman full of joy, knowing that her son, Jim, had followed her word in giving his life to the Lord. And someday we will all be reunited in Heaven. Amen.

Before I go into the Conclusion chapter of Anger Management, allow me to express my sincere sorrow and remorse for taking the life of my victim, Mr. Terrance Kurtz. I often find myself thinking about the crime, and the ripple effect of suffering I caused his family, my family, all officials involved in my incarceration, and all people who were affected by my negative behavior. I am truly sorry.

I thank my loving family, Ernest and Ruth, my parents, Angela, Sharon, Donna, and Judy, my sisters, as well as other family members, for all their support throughout my life and incarceration. And I also thank everyone who has helped me over these thirty four plus years of time in prison. But most importantly, I thank Almighty God for calling me, saving me, preserving me throughout all the years of my life, and for granting me, Victory over Anger!

Conclusion

Anger Management

··

Anger is one of our basic human emotions. It can range from mild irritation to extreme rage. And it can be triggered at any time.

When the emotion of anger is triggered it needs to be managed correctly. For the person who cannot control their anger, is a person who will controlled by their anger. And anger is not an emotion that you want to be in control of your mind. For it can lead to all kinds of negative behavior, including destructive criminal behavior. Indeed, anger has played a part in countless crimes throughout the years of humanity.

If you are a person who knows you have a problem controlling your anger, get in an anger management class as soon as possible. Do not make the same mistake I did, in waiting until it was too late before I got my problems with anger corrected. For it cost a young man his life, and the victim ripple effect of the crime goes far beyond what a person can imagine.

Let me talk to you men for a moment.

As a man, I understand that you do not want to be considered as being a weak individual. I get it. But, the man who cannot control his anger is actually a very weak minded individual. For the Bible says in the book of Proverbs, that the man who cannot control his own spirit (especially his emotion of anger), is like a city without walls. A city without walls back then was very weak.

Are you a person who is constantly in heated arguments, breaking or destroying property, hurting people physically and emotionally? Get in an anger management class. Learn the needed skills to avoid serious problems, situations that can result in consequences which may affect the rest of your life.

The key to effective anger management can be summed up in one word. Forgiveness.

In Paul's letter to the Ephesians, he states;

> "Let all bitterness, and wrath, and anger, and clamor, and evil speaking, be put away from you, with all malice: and be you kind one to another, tenderhearted, **forgiving** one another, even as God for Christ's sake has forgiven you."

The person who chooses to hold onto a grudge of unforgiving anger, such as I did towards my father, is a person who is going to have a problem living peacefully in society. For the anger that is held in the mind through a grudge, is anger that will manifest itself sooner or later. And when it does, it is usually released towards an innocent person who does not deserve the anger.

Effective anger management does not mean you will never get angry. No, that is not realistic. Your emotion of anger is in you for a reason. You just need to learn how to control that anger in the correct way. That is effective anger management.

With the help of Almighty God, we can all be granted;

Victory over Anger

Thank you very much.

Jim

On January 31ˢᵗ, 2024, James Dean Anderson 138154, was granted parole by the Florida Commission on Offender Review. And on February 13ᵗʰ, 2024, James returned to society to live life successfully on parole. Amen

About the Author

James Dean Anderson, a person who went from a life of stability to a homeless teenager, to a young man full of anger and rage, then incarceration for over thirtyfour years. But through it all, God delivered him from the trap of his past, to a glorious walk of salvation.

Printed in the United States
by Baker & Taylor Publisher Services